Welcome to 69 Way's To Please a Chef, a book written by a Chefs and for Chefs!

The book is a tongue in cheek look at the kitchen behaviours ar drive Chefs out of their minds on a regular basis.

We asked Chefs from our online social media group, The Chef Tre ally ground their gears about many aspects of working in a kitchen; from demanding customers, to disappearing General Managers and everything else in between. Their responses form the basis of this book and we hope they give a good insight into the life of a Chef.

Our aim with the book is to first give people who work in a kitchen a laugh, but we also hope non kitchen folk (let's call them civilians) can get an understanding of the trials and tribulations that most Chefs go through.

So if you're a Chef who is banging his head against the wall, why not leave a copy of this book lying around for your General Manager, or Front of House colleagues to read? You never know, they may finally understand just what makes you tick!

For a new way to find great Chef vacancies, check out The Chef Tree web app @ www.thecheftree.com

69 Ways to Please Your Chef

Part 1: The Kitchen

1: Spoons

Everyone loves spoons, right? I like to look at them like tiny little bowls with handles that let me taste what I'm cooking. Without spoons, any kitchen would be in real trouble.
But there are times when I see spoons and I want to kill people. And that time is when they are left in tubs in the fridge.
I mean, what the hell am I meant to think when I see that? Is that a clean spoon or has that been licked, sucked and drooled over by the donkey breathed KP who fancied a go on one of my sauces?
Try my sauce, fine. Just don't leave the spoon in there. Got it?

2: Cling Film

Even as I think about this I can feel my blood start to boil...
Picture the scene; you've had a heavy night on the drink after a busy service. All you want is your bed, so you throw your clothes on the floor and climb into your pit, safe in the knowledge that you can have four or five hours precious sleep before you're back in the kitchen.
Now imagine that someone creeps into your room when you're sleeping and turns all your clothes inside out and ties the arms and legs into knots. When the alarm goes off and you jump up to get dressed, instead of falling calmly into your clothes you've got to go through some insane performance art as you try and work out just how to get dressed.
Well that's just how I feel when some numpty ruins the end of my cling film.

3: No Mise En Place

How do you pack when you go on holiday? Do you run around the place chucking everything into your suitcase, zip the mess up and hope you've remembered everything that you need?

Or do you set everything out before you start packing, knowing you have everything you need, then pack it away all neat and tidy so that if fits into your suitcase?

If you're in the first camp, stay away from my kitchen and best wishes when you get lucky on holiday (because Chefs always get lucky on holiday) and are looking for your contraception, because it ain't there. It's on the bedside table at home because you are an unorganised chump. And now you ain't getting any.

That's how it is with mise en place. Set it out nicely before you begin and life in the kitchen will be smooth.

4: Radio Stations

Messing with a Chefs radio station is like wearing someone else's underwear. You just don't do it. If I'm on my feet for 14 hours every day, I want to listen to my tunes. It's what gets me through the shift.

If I come in and someone has tuned into Twat FM and I have to listen to some crazy 160 bpm trance/garage/grunge fusion mix, I'm likely to get a little stabby during service.

If you want to choose the radio station, put the years in and earn your stripes. Until then, I'm in charge of the tunes. And you can call me DJ Billy Con Carne.

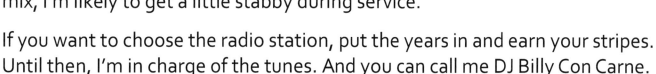

5: The Kitchen Pen

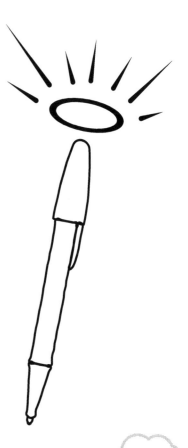

Everyone who has ever worked in a professional kitchen knows that there is an ancient law, passed down from a time long past and protected by wizards and elves, that means a kitchen can only ever have one pen. You can have a dozen or more knives for every eventuality but you are only ever allowed one pen.

Therefore, if you use the 'Gilded Pen of Avalon', make sure you leave it where everyone else can get access to it. You can of course leave the pen behind your ear but I will likely come for it wielding an extremely sharp knife that I use exclusively for de-boning pigs' trotters. You have been warned.

6: Moaning about breaks

I'll be wrestling with five or six different dishes, trying not to melt into a grease spot as my core temperature mimics the uranium tubes at my local nuclear power station, when some annoying FOH will start moaning about not having had a break all service.

And as the FOH gets closer I get the unmistakeable whiff of a recently extinguished cigarette...

You haven't had a break but you've managed to consume god knows how many oily rags while I've been dealing with a really bad case of Chefs Arse all service.

Like the geezer in Reservoir Dogs says, 'here's the world's smallest violin playing just for the waitresses.'

7: Getting Phone Calls During Service

Everyone who knows me, knows I'm a Chef. I don't have to tell them, they know it because I am always in the kitchen and can never, ever, make it for that drink/meal out/footie match/christening/ wedding/funeral, etc, etc, etc. My life is based completely around the four walls of this kitchen.
So why are you phoning me during service? What do you expect me to do…'Hello mate, lovely to hear from you, I'll let these steaks burn so we can discuss just how rubbish our football team is'…
I don't phone you when you're earning your living, so please, don't phone me.
The only exception to this is when you call me to tell me my numbers have come up on the Lottery.

8: Clean As You Go (CAYG)

You don't have to tell me that a kitchen is a busy place because I'm at the front line. But that doesn't excuse you not cleaning up as you go along. It only takes a few seconds to wipe down and put stuff away. You might be busy but so are the rest of us and whoever comes along next time is going to have to clean up your mess.

If you leave it looking like the aftermath of a T.K Maxx clothing sale then that's just making life harder for the rest of us.

9: Staff Turning up Late and Hungover

A professional kitchen is one of the most stressful environments there is, outside of an operating theatre and a conflict zone, and I understand why people need to let off steam every now and again. But I'm going to have a problem with you if it's happening on a regular basis.

A kitchen is only as good as the team that works there and if you're turning up late and hungover all the time, you're not helping the team. It's unprofessional and disrespectful to the rest of the team who will have to carry you when you turn up to work like a wrung out tea towel.

Save it for your day(s) off, right?

10: Do not touch MY knife

It may not look like much to you, but my knife is a thing of beauty. Just like you know when you've found the right partner, a Chef knows when they've found the right knife. And hopefully, both will stay with you forever. And just as you wouldn't mess with a mate's partner, you'd better not mess with a Chef's knife. In fact, I've known Chefs who'd rather you messed with their partner than their knife. But they had some serious issues.

And don't even think about putting my blade in the dishwasher. You are not helping me out, you're making my life even worse than it already is.

11: Sales Reps turning up during service.

You work in this industry, right? You know the times of service for most restaurants are the same the world over, right?

So why come into my place during service and expect me to spend time chewing the fat about what my kitchen needs. During service, my kitchen needs me!

So the next time it happens, expect a visit from me in the near future. I'll come in when you're in the middle of an important meeting with your boss, and I'll expect you to listen to what I have to say.

YOU'RE NOT BUSY, ARE YOU?

Hell, just like you take food off of plates as you leave, I'll take a couple of pens on my way out. Won't be able to put them in the kitchen though, the pen wizards would have something to say about that.

12: Staff on their Phones

I get that people these days are connected and we live in an online community. That many of us live our lives through social media and are defined by the number of friends or followers we have and by the number of likes we generate.

I don't have a problem with that at all. But I do have a problem when my staff are hitting up their phones when they should be hitting up their prep.

Your life is not that important that you need to check in or check up every five minutes.

Save it for your multiple fag breaks...

13: Washing up still there in the morning.

If you want to make a Chef's heart soar, then leave a pile of washing up from the night before.

Because we love it when people tell us they're going to do something and then completely go back on their word and leave it for someone else to do. It's why we get up in the mornings...to be greeted by a massive pile of dirty dishes. Who wouldn't love that, eh?

So next time you tell me you'll do the washing up and leave it, I'll do the same when you ask me to feed you.

14: Not Putting Items Back Where They Belong

I'm a firm believer in 'a place for everything, everything in its place'. A kitchen runs like a well (olive) oiled machine and when you need something, it needs to be there.

Imagine if you took your car for a service and as you entered the workshop the mechanics were running around looking for tools. Would you think that this would be a good place to leave your car? Or would you be thinking, 'I'm not leaving my pride and joy with these clueless clowns'?

A kitchen can be a dangerous place during service. The last thing you want is someone running around looking for a utensil or tool that isn't where it should be.

15: Not Cleaning a Messy Workstation

Just like CAYG (cleaning as you go), clearing a messy workstation should be second nature to anyone working in a kitchen.

If someone has to use a messy workstation then you're opening up the kitchen to cross contamination as well as allergy issues.

When you've finished, take a moment to wipe down PROPERLY. Put yourself in the position of the person who has to use that space next. Would you like to be greeted by an explosion in an offal factory when you come to use that workstation?

By leaving a messy workplace, you're putting the whole team under pressure as they have to clear up after you.

16: Kitchen No Shows

We've all been here. There's been a night out; someone's birthday or what not, and the whole team has been out to celebrate. The next morning, when you're all stood around, nursing hangovers and mouths as dry as a tramp's bath matt, there's usually one no show.

One of the crew who couldn't even drag themselves out of their pit to phone and let you know that they're a lightweight.

So the team has to pick up the slack and fill in for the no show, and somehow get to the end of service in one piece. Cheers mate, thanks for that.

Depending on the individual, I'll tolerate it once, maybe twice.

But just remember, there is a cruel and unusual justice in a professional kitchen. And you've just been proven guilty of a terrible crime. The punishment is on its way, when you least expect it.

17: Finishing the Last of Anything and not telling anyone

Or maybe they'll leave a single, solitary molecule of an ingredient and tell you they thought I could use it.

The main reason people do this is because they can't be bothered to add the item to the order list.

There is nothing more frustrating than reaching for an ingredient in the walk in and finding the box suspiciously light. You know it's empty but did they really think you wouldn't notice?

This is the kitchen equivalent of finding, after a night spent at the local Indian, only one sheet of paper left on the toilet roll.

I hope I've captured the trials and tribulations of being a Chef in a kitchen. It's a tough job but you wouldn't do it if you didn't love it, right?

You might not feel the love every day, but when you produce a great plate of food, there's no better feeling.

I'm all for Chefs blowing their own trumpet and letting people know just how great they are. It's great to really impress a customer or a fellow Chef.

One way to do this is by taking great photos of the food you make and getting them out there for all to see. Banging photos out on Facebook or Instagram is a great way to sell yourself and your kitchen.

We have a free photo guide e-book available with loads of great tips on how to make your images as good as they can be. Happy snapping, Chefs!

http://www.thecheftree.com/food-photo-guide/

Part 2: Customers

18: Walking in 10 minutes before the end of service

...and expecting a full menu to be available.

Come on, think about it. You don't tip up to the cinema once a film has started and expect the projectionist to rewind the film for you, do you?

The restaurant has gone through a full service and a lot of items are likely to be sold out. Plus my team have started to pack away and are hoping they might finally get to see their nearest and dearest when they're not sound asleep.

CAN YOU SQUEEZE US IN?

We stay open to ten pm, so I'll cook you something, just don't expect the world, 'cos that just sold out.

Anyway, did no one tell you how unhealthy it is to eat so late?

19: Well Done Steak

A particular favourite of Chefs who appreciate the beauty and taste of a good piece of meat.

Cooking steak well done is a little bit like putting fluffy dice in your Ferrari. You can do it but everyone is going to think you have all the taste of an extra from TOWIE.

I know this is all about personal preference but I don't think people that eat steak well done have ever tried it any other way. Steak should never be cooked beyond medium (and even then, some of you will be twitching). That beautiful piece of meat will taste of nothing but charcoal. Did Bessie the Aberdeen Angus really give her life for this? Time to mooove on...

STILL A BIT RARE?!!!

20: Waste

If a half-eaten plate of food comes back to the kitchen because of a problem, I can put it right. I might not agree with the customer's analysis of the problem but I will give them what they want.

When a half-eaten plate comes back because the customer didn't want to eat it, then my hackles rise like a river at the bottom of the Yorkshire Dales. Me and the team have sweated (not literally) over that plate of food and you, it seems, can't be bothered to eat it.

Why not? I'd rather you made a ridiculous complaint than just left it there, untouched and unloved, destined for the waste bin (or the KP's lunch box). It's a bit of a kick in the teeth for us, like you can't dignify our efforts by actually consuming what you ordered just a little while ago.

21: Allergies

What is going on with the world? Since the end of the Second World War, science and medicine has managed to eradicate most diseases that had previously killed millions across the planet. Life expectancy around the world has increased. The humans that inhabit the planet have become much stronger and resilient than at any other time in history.

It seems we can withstand the most virulent disease and illness but when confronted with a piece of wheat, some sections of society are unable to cope. We've become so tolerant of so much and yet, in the last 20 years, we've become intolerant of every food type on the planet. How did this happen?

I'm not disputing that some people do genuinely suffer from allergies and intolerances. It just seems that the numbers of people are far too high.

Next time you refuse that piece of bread, ask yourself if you really are gluten intolerant or if bread just makes you fart a lot!

22: Buy your lovely Chef a beer

We don't ask for much back here in the kitchen. We toil away in the heat and the pressure of the kitchen whilst our more pretty (and less psychotic) colleagues (FOH, I'm looking at you) get much of the credit (as well as the bloody tips!) for your dining experience.

They say money makes the world go around but in a hot kitchen, our currency is more liquid.

Send a beer back to the kitchen and we will love you forever. And next time you come in, you'll be well looked after.

23: If you see your Chef, say thanks

Linked to 22, this one. Everybody likes to be praised for the job they do. No one is going to look at you like you're a lunatic for saying, 'thanks, mate, you did a great job'.

Try it with your bin people. Next time you see them picking up the rubbish, drop a 'thank you' on them. It will make their day and I bet they start putting the bins back in the right place!

Chefs are human too, and we like to be thanked for a job well done. Again, a small effort goes a long way.

24: Don't Ask for Salt, the Chef tasted it

We are trained, believe it or not, to have good taste buds. The dish we deliver to your table has been seasoned exactly as it should be.

So it really irks us Chefs when we look out to see customers pouring salt all over the plate before they've even tasted their meal. You might like a lot of salt but the dish you eat will not thank you for it, and neither will your Chef.

So please, don't disrespect the Chef by chucking a load of salt all over that lovingly prepared dish. It's not good for your, or the Chef's blood pressure.

25: Threatening us with Trip Advisor

Okay, sometimes thing go wrong in the kitchen and your experience might not be as good as you expected. Let us know, right away, and we'll try and resolve it.

Please, please, don't threaten to leave us a negative review on Trip Advisor. It makes you look like an idiot and any goodwill from us will go out of the window.

Look, most people who use Trip Advisor can spot the people trying it on. If a restaurant has consistently good reviews, and then gets a random bad one, it suggests that this person is trying it on to get a free meal.

And beware the response from the restaurant. A witty retort from the restaurant can end up going viral and making the customer look an even bigger tool.

26: Calorie counters/fussy eaters

We are in the hospitality industry. We are not a nursery school, ready to cater to your every whim. If you're counting calories or are a fussy eater, why not just stay at home and have a nice glass of water, rather than try and make my delicious food more acceptable to your finicky palate?

We understand that some people take the food they consume very seriously, and fair play to them if it makes them feel better about themselves. But when you go out to eat, the responsibility for your food is now out of your hands and in the hands of the kitchen. So relax a little. You never know, you may actually enjoy yourself.

27: Letting children run riot

I know that Amelia and Sebastian are the apple of your eye, but please, you're out in a civilised restaurant, don't let them run amok, just so you can finish your meal in peace.

I embrace children in restaurants (not literally, of course), and I think more restaurants should welcome younger diners. But this is a two way street. If we welcome your children, please be so kind as to keep an eye on them.

Not only do rowdy children ruin the experience of other diners, but a restaurant can be a dangerous place, with hot food and drinks everywhere. I'm sure a trip to A&E would ruin your night a lot more than it would ours.

28: Ordering off menu

There is an unspoken agreement between a restaurant and its customers. We will spend time and effort creating a menu we hope you will enjoy. You, in turn, will order, from said menu, what you would like to eat.

Just because we are a kitchen, and therefore have ingredients, doesn't mean we will cook you anything you fancy. That doesn't work in restaurants.

"DARLING THEY DON'T HAVE AVACADO AND QUAIL'S EGGS"

But I'll tell you where it does work. At home. So why not toddle off home and make whatever it is you fancy at this moment. Because I'm not going to make it for you in my kitchen.

29: Needy Customers

Those people who monopolise the time of the FOH staff with their whiny voices and their indecisions.

You know the ones. Those people that think the whole world revolves around them and their quest for the perfect night out. See those other tables full of people? They're customers as well and they manage to enjoy themselves without bending the ear of all of the staff in the place with their ridiculous demands.

This is not a therapy session, it's a meal. You think you've got it bad, come in the back and meet the KP who lives in a shoe.

30: Serial Complainers

They can be the bane of our lives and every restaurant gets them from time to time. Those people, that no matter what you do for them, will complain about absolutely everything. They usually start from the moment they walk through the door;

 'This chair is too low/high.'

'Why is it so noisy in here?'

'Why is this plate round?'

Why did the Chef just stab me in the eye?'

You would think, that with countless television channels available, that these people would just stay at home and shout at the goggle box. But no, they have to attempt to infect everyone else with the misery virus. Enough.

31. Eating three quarters of a meal and then asking for a refund

If it takes you that long to discover that you don't like the food, I suggest that you might be dead already. And if you don't get the hell out of my restaurant, I can guarantee that you soon will be. Along with the Trip Advisor warriors, this type of customer really grinds my gears. They are so obviously trying it on to get a free meal. This is one customer you really want to lose.

THANKS FOR THE FREE MEAL SUCKA!

I hope I haven't gone too far with my thoughts on customers!

We all know that some customers can offer more 'challenges' than others but at the end of the day, the customers that come through the doors are the life-blood of any restaurant.

Over on our blog page, we've got some great posts about how to handle customers, as well as some great articles about all things kitchen. If you like this book, you'll love our blogs!

http://www.thecheftree.com/blog

Part 3: FOH Staff

32. Leaving food on the hot plate

See that congealing mess of once beautiful ingredients, lovingly sourced from the finest suppliers and put together by mine own hands, hands that would right now like to be around your throat? That **_was_** someone's dinner. Now I have to start again, just because the customer wasn't one of your tables.

I appreciate that the job you do is highly skilled and extremely exhausting but how about taking one for the team every now and again and just taking the food out to the table? It won't kill you...and if you help me out, neither will I.

33. Clear your plates at pot wash

So I've got my hands full with a pan of boiling water that really needs putting down before I drop the bugger.

But as I stagger over to the pot wash I realise that FOH have started another really important game of 'Plate Jenga' and there is no room whatsoever to put this beast down. CRASSSH...

Come on, is it really that difficult to clear the plates and stack them up neatly? Next time it happens I'm loosening the tops on the condiments and we'll play my game of 'Salt Roulette'. Spin the wheel, baby!

34. Let us know when you use something up

If you've used the last butter portion, or sent out the last truffle, do me a favour, let me know.

Just like the cling film issue, finding an empty box of anything is extremely frustrating, because if I'm looking for it, it generally means that I need it. All you had to do was tell me and I could have ordered more.

Despite the bald head I am not Professor X from the X-Men and I am unable to read minds.

I'm pretty good at reading the riot act, though.

* NOT PSYCHIC

35: Don t Stand Around Chatting

BLAH, BLAH BLAH, BLAH...

Unless you're my significant other, I really don't care about who you slept with last night.

I'm also not at all interested in how many pints/shots you drank, where you went dancing or any of that myriad of nonsense that seems to make up the lifestyle of most F.O.H staff. I'm a Chef, and I'm grumpy, I don't need to be reminded that other people have a life, especially when it's busy.

When the kitchen is rushing around trying to get out the orders that you took, it's really galling to see you relaxing and chewing the cud with your friends. Instead, why not do the right thing and...

36: Offer to Help

As the saying goes, there is no I in team. And at the end of the day, that is what we are.

And when we all pull together, FOH and BOH, working as one finely tuned kitchen machine, it is indeed a thing of beauty and wonder.

We may, at times, hate and despise our FOH colleagues, but deep in the depths of our souls we know that we couldn't do it without them. But before I get too touchy feely I must continue to point out the many ways in which FOH annoy Chefs...

37: Have some Banter with the Kitchen

BANTS MATE
INNIT?!

Banter is the oxygen that Chefs breathe. It is the thing that gets us through the long and busy shifts in the kitchen.

Basically, we like to take the piss. Having a laugh (at someone's expense, usually) takes us out of the kitchen for a moment, and reminds us that we do enjoy what we do from time to time.

So, FOH, don't get upset by our ways, join in and have a bit of banter with the kitchen crew. If you're **standoffish** with us, the banter only increases.

38: Have some more Banter

Did I say we like banter already?

If you want to earn your stripes with the kitchen brigade, come on in and give us a bit of lip every now and again. It shows us that you've got the guts to survive in the kitchen environment.

If you can walk into our domain and actively take the piss out of us, you'll get our utmost respect and admiration. We see banter like a game of tennis, the 'banter ball' needs to get returned to really enjoy the game.

39: Bring Coffee

Like banter is the oxygen we breathe, so coffee is the fuel we have to take on to keep going. So if you bring us regular doses of coffee, you're actually helping run the kitchen.

Don't be afraid to keep it coming, we can never have enough coffee.

Even if we're red faced and wild eyed, frothing at the mouth in the middle of a caffeine overdose, we always need more coffee.

Until we're dead. Then you can stop bringing coffee. Thanks.

40: Bring Cold Drinks

See 39.

In the summer, when the temperature in the kitchen is hotter than inside the rational, and we're all sweating like two rats rutting in a wool sock, you'll need to supplement the coffee with cold drinks.

Ice and a slice shows you really care. A cold beer tells us that you love us really.

41: Tips

Those notes and coins you share out amongst your FOH friends (and usually our lovely GM), any chance we could have some of that? I know you look lovely and have nice manners, but we do play quite an active role in this whole cooking/eating thing.

I mean, I wouldn't ask but it appears that we toiled to prepare that amazing food you walked out to the table and put down in front of the customer.

A good rule to remember in a professional kitchen is, 'Look after the Chef, and he will look after you'.

So when you're getting a hard time from a customer who has been waiting all of five minutes for their starters, I can help with that…

42: FOH Mistakes

Experienced FOH staff rarely make mistakes. The problem is, experienced FOH staff are as rare as rocking horse shit. Instead, the majority of FOH are our future leaders of government, industry, finance and the world. I am of course talking about students.

How some of these bedsit scholars manage to talk and walk at the same time is sometimes a mystery to me. They might be able to knock out a 30,000 word essay on 'Symbolism and Metaphors in the Lyrics of Justin Bieber' (actual essay title – probably), but they sometimes seem incapable of writing a four word food order.

Don't look for hidden meanings in the menu, there are none. Just take the order and write it so we can read it. You can write like an exploded octopus when you qualify as a GP.

43: FOH Breaks

Breaks? Remind me what those are again?

I appreciate that carrying plates from the kitchen to a table, fetching drinks and condiments and smiling AT ALL TIMES can be extremely taxing after an early life of mummy and daddy taking care of your every need, but come on. Do you really need that many breaks?

And what really grips my shit is that some FOH will take a break directly after standing around talking about who they slept with last night.

And if FOH don't get a break because it's really busy, well, you never hear the end of that.

Take heed from another Chef motto, 'I'll take a break when I drop down dead'.

44: Bad Table Management

See that bit out there, where all the customers sit, that's the front of house. That is your responsibility, your area of control. Me and the kitchen crew take care of back of house.

So when you get a rush out front, please think about how you send in your orders. Remember to stagger the orders that come into the kitchen. Because one way to upset your kitchen, as well as your customers, is to swamp the kitchen with orders.

Be honest with the customer if you know it's busy and let them know there is going to be a wait. It saves a lot of hassle for you further down the line.

45: Rushing your Chef

EMULSION YOU SAY?

Just like Rome wasn't built in a day, this Pan Seared Snail Kidney on a Bed of Foraged Nettles with an Essence of Elderberry Reduction can in no way, ever, be rushed.

This is what I do, and I know better than you how to do it.

Imagine if they would have rushed Michelangelo as he painted the Sistine Chapel;

'C'mon Mike, it's been four years already. Can't you just use a bit of matt emulsion on that last little bit? No one's going to notice?'

I wouldn't expect you to go out with half your clothes on so don't ask me to send a dish that isn't ready.

46. Asking for food during service

If I'm sweating like a Chef hard at work in a kitchen, then please don't bother asking me to rustle you up a lovingly prepared meal. Those people called customers, who you should be looking after, rather than badgering me for food, are actually paying for the privilege of me cooking for them. They are my priority.

And anyway, what the hell are you doing eating food during service?

And if I see you pick something off a plate that is waiting to go out, I'll likely go for your fingers with my blade. You handle money and money is filthy. They call it 'dirty money' for a reason.

Ask me nicely when I'm not so busy and I might help you out but not if you give me a…

47: Fussy staff meal request

You know the one. You've just finished morning prep and then the rest of the 'team' turn up expecting to be fed. Which is not usually a problem until you hear;

"Could I have a burger but can you make sure the beef is halal and I'd like it on a half brioche, half bagel with organic cucumber strips and some low fat, mayonnaise free coleslaw. And give it to me well done..."

I don't do it for the customers, and they pay my wages, so I sure as hell won't be doing it for you.

48: Don't ask me silly questions

If you're new to the kitchen or to being FOH, I'll help you out as much as I can but please, think about some of the things you ask me before you open your mouth.

"Can you make the dish without oyster mushrooms as the customer is allergic to seafood."

"The customer is on a diet, could you make the beurre noisette without butter, please."

And let's not forget the classic;

"Can you make an eggless omelette, Chef?"

49: Binning Cutlery

When you finally get round to scraping the plate, try and make sure that the cutlery is removed beforehand and not just dump the whole lot into the bin. I mean, it's quite difficult to dump cutlery isn't it? Seeing how it looks nothing like food and makes a loud noise when it goes in the bin.

Cutlery is expensive as well as being incredibly useful for most restaurants.

Also, we might have to go through the bins for some reason and it's really not great to come back up with a knife or fork embedded in your hand.

50: Know the Menu

Think of the menu as the blueprint for how we do our jobs. We use the menu day in and day out but our customers do not. The least you can do is learn what the menu items are so you can impart your wisdom to the customer when they ask what is in the dish.

It doesn't look professional when you have to scamper back to the kitchen to find out about a dish that you've been serving for the last week. So take some time to find out about the dish and ask me questions before it goes on the menu.

51: Getting the order wrong

You spoke to the customer, asked them what they wanted to eat, how they wanted it and then made a note of it, right? You passed that note to the kitchen and we followed it and produced the meal as requested.

So how come two minutes after it goes out, the order comes back because it's wrong. Where did this simple process break down, I wonder? 'Cos it sure as hell wasn't with us.

And don't think we don't know what you tell the customer out front, putting the blame on the kitchen. 'Yeah, it's really busy back there, Chef is getting a little stressed.'

Damn right I'm getting stressed when my FOH can't take down a simple order.

So, in future, remember to repeat the customer's order back to them if you're not sure just what they ordered.

52: Putting dirty plates in the sink

If you do this, pretty soon you're going to have a really disgusting soup of every ingredient that went out of the kitchen.

It's unhygienic and some poor sod is going to have to get their hand in there to sort it out.

So take a moment to scrape the food off the plate before you dump it down for the KP to sort out.

If you don't, the next time it happens I may well take a sample and heat it up for you the next time you ask me for some food.

There must be a restaurant somewhere that has a harmonious relationship between FOH and the kitchen. I'd love to go there because I expect they'll have Dodo on the menu!

I hope in some small way this book will help FOH and Chef relationships. If I could end the war between the two I'd probably win the Nobel Peace Prize.

For some more posts about the love lost between FOH and kitchens, check out our social media page - https://www.facebook.com/groups/TheChefTree/ - where you'll also find lots of useful stuff about Cheffing, alongside a load of banter and some horror stories about kitchen life.

Part 4: Days Off

53: Getting the "quick call"

You know the 'quick call', right?

"Hello Chef, just a quick call to ask you..."

And it is never, ever just a quick call. I'll end up on speaker phone dishing out orders to the team and it will be like I'm there, in amongst the heat, the sweat and the stress. The only difference being I'll be in my underwear and not my whites.

Please, don't call me on my day off. It's a chance for me to get drunk and take a dump, possibly at the same time.

54: Don't ask me to cook for you

If you have any friends that work in the trades (builders, sparks, chippies etc.) have you ever noticed that when you go to their house, it's always in a bit of a state; half finished jobs, tools lying around, that kind of thing?

That's because that when you work hard at something all day, the last thing you want to do is come back home and start again.

If you worked in a clothing store and came round to my place, wouldn't you be a little pissed off if I asked you to come and fold all my clothes and arrange them in a neat and orderly fashion?

So please, don't ask me to cook for you on my day off.

55: Friends suggestions

With so many cooking shows on the telly and food blogs on the internet, the world and his life partner have an opinion about food and how it should be put together.

The world doesn't work like that though. When I watch 'Murder She Wrote' on a quiet Sunday, I don't immediately phone up Scotland Yard and offer my services to catch the latest serial killer that's on the loose.

So please, keep your suggestions to yourself and remember that opinions are like arseholes; everyone has one.

56: Being scared to cook for me

Are you kidding? I love it when anyone offers to cook for me. I consider it a rare treat that my nearest and dearest would spend the time and effort to create a wonderful meal for me.

Look, just because I spend all day doing this, making sure that every dish that goes out of my kitchen is the best it can possibly be, enduring long hours and pretty terrible pay, alongside burns, cuts and a really bad case of Chefs arse, doesn't make me cynical about the food anyone puts in front of me. No way, I appreciate each and every effort of cooking that is put in front of me. Because I'm a nice guy.*

Unless it tastes like shit. If it tastes like shit you're gonna get it without mercy and with both barrels.

57: Question: Do you like to cook?

Answer: No, I'm in the business for the glamour, the comfortable and stress free working environment, the short hours and incredible pay.

A bit like asking Harry Styles if he likes to wear tight jeans. The answer is fairly obvious I would say.

All Chefs like to cook. Some of us love to cook. It's all the crap in between the cooking that makes us a little 'frustrated'.

The expression 'work hard, play hard' must have been written by a Chef. Chefs tend to make the most of any time away from the kitchen. Probably because they don't know when they'll get another day off!

But these days, having a good work/life balance is important. Far too many Chefs work far too many hours, sometimes for far too little pay.

If you're in that category, maybe it's time to take stock of things before you hit the buffers.

Over on our web app - http://app.thecheftree.com/ - you'll find a load of new and exciting Chef opportunities. The great thing about our app is that you can choose the hours you want to work and your hourly rate so you can get that work/life balance right.

Part 5: Management/Owners

58: Communicate with your Chef

We know you have a busy business to run but the kitchen is the engine room of every restaurant and that means that your kitchen brigade is on the front line of your business.

If something isn't working, speak to your Chef before you make changes that may not be needed or may have a negative impact on the business or employees.

Don't just poke your head into the kitchen when you have a problem and need to vent your anger.

We won't take you seriously and you'll lose all of our respect.

59: Big Bookings

Do us a favour when you take a large booking, get a pre-order. And well you're at it, get a name with each dish, because everyone forgets what they originally ordered.

Your kitchen doesn't need any more stress so whatever you can do to help us will come back and help you in the long run.

60: Take Outs

The polystyrene take away box is the nemesis of the Chef. It's not that you won't find one in our hands from time to time, usually as we stagger back from the pub or club as we make the most of a rare night off.

But Chefs don't make fast food, they make food that has been thought out, structured, considered and then lovingly prepared. The poly box is the complete opposite.

So when a manager or owner asks me to cook a meal and dump it in a box so a customer can take it away, I can't help but recoil in horror.

What message does that send out to the customers in the restaurant, as you walk through with a poly box in your hands?

I'm better than that, and so should you be.

61: Say Thank you and really mean it

Any Chef worth his salt takes pride in the food he sends out. They might not like the pay, the working hours, the conditions or even you, but they will work their arse off to make sure the kitchen runs as smoothly as possible.

Saying thank you every now and again shows us that you do appreciate the efforts we make for you.

We don't expect a pat on the back for the work you pay us to do but a small appreciation goes a very long way. As does...

62: Beer

Buy your Chef a beer after service every now and again, especially after he's worked his nuts off and got you out of the shit again. Better still, have a beer with them and get to know what really makes them tick.

Having a beer and a chat might also help a Chef get to know his owner/manager a bit better.

As the saying possibly goes, 'Beer, the cause of...and solution to...all of life's problems.'

63. Schedule Regular Meetings

Not just with your Chef but with all your employees. If we feel that lines of communication are open, we're more likely to speak to you about issues and problems we are having. If you don't speak to us, chances are we're not going to care about the business very much.

Speaking to your staff is a chance to get a different perspective on your business as well as finding out what they need to perform their job better.

Ask your staff for suggestions on how to improve. It's your business but we know everything that is going on from the ground up.

If you have a problem, involve us in finding solutions.

64. Give the Chef five minutes

Sometimes, when it's all kicking off in the kitchen, the Chef needs a space to sort their head out, a chance to see the wood for the trees.

Giving your Chef five minutes to reset themselves is a lot more productive than trying to push through the fog of a really hectic service.

Your Chef will come back to the kitchen with a clearer vision of what they need to do to get the ship back on course.

65: Lazy managers

Just because the place is running smoothly doesn't mean there isn't something you should be doing.

The rest of the employees look to the manager as a lead on how to behave. If we're all working hard while the manager is swanning around, then pretty soon things are going to come to a head.

Not only will you have lost the respect of the team, but morale will plummet, productivity will drop through the floor and staff will start to leave.

If you haven't got anything else to do, pitch in with helping out elsewhere.

But best stay out of my kitchen; I'm the guv'nor in there.

66: Poor Rotas

There is nothing quite as frustrating as turning up to work to find that half of your brigade have been given the day off when you know it's about to go crazy bat shit mental. You end up being as busy as a one legged man in an ass kicking contest when all that pressure could have been prevented by a decent, well thought out rota.

The flip side of this is when you know it's going to be quiet and you turn up for work and the kitchen is packed tighter than an Aussie lifeguard's budgie smugglers. There's a reason why they say, 'too many cooks spoil the broth'.

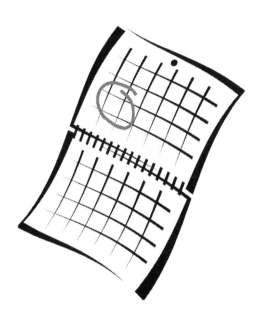

67. Make up your mind

If you're going to go to the trouble of telling us things are changing, make sure you've thought it through before the big announcement.

We'll pretty much go along with most things you ask us to do but when you start dithering about things and changing your mind then you're starting to really piss us off.

So have the courage of your convictions and make the change stick.

68. Where have you gone?

Sometimes, trying to find a manager in a busy restaurant is like playing a real life game of 'Where's Wally'. No matter how hard you look, you just can't find them.

Some managers have the ability to disappear quicker than a fart in a fan factory, usually when the brown stuff is about to hit the same fan.

I don't know where they go, I don't have the time to look for them. Maybe they have a panic room where they go and stroke their unicorns when the pace gets too demanding.

69. Treat me as an equal

You might have the fancy title and get to wear the shiny shoes but don't think for one minute that you're better than me.

I've trained for years to get to this position. Worked my way up with hard work, dedication and determination because I really love what I do. Respect that and we'll get along fine.

Treat me like one of your minions and I'll get my coat and walk. My skills are extremely transferable so I won't sweat losing this job because I know I'll find somewhere that will look after me.

Can you say the same thing?

So there you go, our 69 ways to keep your Chef happy. It's not that hard, is it?

I hope you've found my book humorous, insightful but must importantly a useful tool to make sure your Chef is kept happy.

It's been proven that a happy Chef is 36% more productive, which means the food goes out correct, hot and on time. So if your Chef is happy, your customers are happy.

Don't forget you can learn more about Chefs and what makes them tick in our online communities on Facebook and Twitter.

Remember to say hello and let me know what you thought of this book.

Pete ;)

Printed in Great Britain
by Amazon